# Learning to Read and Write
# Step by Step!

### Ready to Read and Write  Preschool–Kindergarten
• big type and easy words
• picture clues
• drawing and first writing activities

For children who like to "tell" stories by drawing pictures and are eager to write.

### Reading and Writing with Help  Preschool–Grade 1
• basic vocabulary
• short sentences
• simple writing activities

For children who use letters, words, and pictures to tell stories.

### Reading and Writing on Your Own  Grades 1–3
• popular topics
• easy-to-follow plots
• creative writing activities

For children who are comfortable writing simple sentences on their own.

**STEP INTO READING® Write-In Readers** are designed to give every child a successful reading and writing experience. The grade levels are only guides. Children can progress through the steps at their own speed, developing confidence in their abilities, no matter what grade.

Remember, a lifetime love of reading and writing starts with a single step!

*To Bennett, with wishes for lots of big ideas!*
*Love and bear hugs from Grandma—K.E.H.*

*To Cindy, my "little sister," no matter how old*
*you get! Love you, xo—D.K.H.*

*To Caroline, with love—Uncle R.W.*

Text copyright © 2005 by Kathryn Heling and Deborah Hembrook. Illustrations copyright
© 2005 by Richard Walz. All rights reserved under International and Pan-American Copyright
Conventions. Published in the United States by Random House Children's Books, a division of
Random House, Inc., New York, and simultaneously in Canada by Random House of Canada
Limited, Toronto.

www.stepintoreading.com

Educators and librarians, for a variety of teaching tools, visit us at
www.randomhouse.com/teachers

Library of Congress Control Number: 2005924078

ISBN: 0-375-83391-9

Printed in the United States of America   10 9 8 7 6 5 4 3 2 1   First Edition

STEP INTO READING, RANDOM HOUSE, and the Random House colophon are registered trademarks
of Random House, Inc.

# BEAR'S BIG IDEAS

## A Write-In Reader

by Kathryn Heling and Deborah Hembrook and

your name

illustrated by Richard Walz and

MULFORD

your name

Random House New York

## Rrrr! Rrrr! Rrrr!

Bear's tummy
is growling.
Bear is hungry.
He is hungry for fish.

Bear calls his friends
with a big idea.

Bear brings a saw.

Buck grabs a hammer.

Moose carries some wood.

# What other tools will they need?

Zuzz, zuzz, zuzz.

Bear saws the wood.

Thump, thump, thump.

Buck hammers the frame.

Shhh, shhh, shhh.

Moose sands it smooth.

The work is done.

It is a boat!

"Now we can fish!"

says Bear.

Bear finds
the fishing poles.

# Buck gets a net.

## Moose digs for worms.

Help Bear and his friends get to the lake.

START HERE

Go over the __bridge__.

Go around the __rocks__.

You will see the __lake__!

The boat floats!

"Off we go!" says Bear

with a great big push.

Moose catches a fish.

Bear hooks an old boot.

Buck catches a fish.

Bear hooks a tire.

"I do not want a boot.

I do not want a tire!

I want fish!"

growls Bear.

"Poor hungry Bear,"
says Buck.
"Keep trying, Bear,"
says Moose.

Bear casts his line again.

He has a bite!

He tugs! He pulls!

At last,
Bear catches
a big, big fish!

Bear loves
to eat fish.
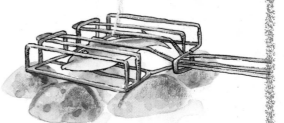

What do <u>you</u> love to eat?

The friends fish
all summer.
Bear gets fat.

Before long,
Bear is ready
for a nap.

# What is Bear dreaming of?

# Rrrr! Rrrr! Rrrr!

Bear's tummy
is growling.
Bear wakes up.

He calls his friends.

"Time to fish again!"

Buck brings the boat.

Moose gets the gear.

The water turned to ice!

"Look," says Bear.

"The boat will not go."

Bear slips.

Buck flips.

Moose flops.

Bear has a new idea.

The friends go to work.

Zuzz, zuzz, zuzz.

Thump, thump, thump.

Shhh, shhh, shhh.

The friends build
a little shack.
It is called an ice shanty.

MULFORD

The work is done!
"The ice shanty
will keep us warm
while we fish,"
says Bear.

The friends cut holes

in the ice.

They drop in

their lines.

Moose catches
a big fish.

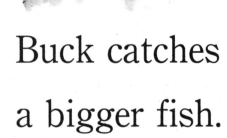

Buck catches
a bigger fish.

Bear catches
the biggest fish of all!

Bear has a full tummy
again.

It is time to go home.

Good night, Bear.

See you in the spring!